The Last Breath of a Love

Sagor sarker

Published by Sagor Sarker, 2024.

THE LAST BREATH OF A LOVE

First edition. November 12, 2024.

ISBN: 979-8230831228

Written by Sagor sarker.

Also by Sagor sarker

The Poetry of Lover's Heart
The Rise of Darkness
Love in Quiet Tremors
The Last Breath of a Love
Embrace Of Sweet Tomorrows
A Smile of Betrayal- A Novel

Watch for more at https://www.facebook.com/sagor.sarker.334/.

Table of Contents

The Last Breath of a Love

When Hearts Speak in Silence

In the stillness, where words fall short, two people can somehow speak without speaking. Sitting side by side in a quiet room, they feel more connected than ever, even as they both know their time together is ending. The silence between them is full, filled with all the things they've shared—every laugh, every touch, and every memory. She holds his hand, and he gently squeezes hers back. There's no need for words because their silence says it all: *I love you. I always will.*

Love like this doesn't just fade. Even when words aren't spoken, it stays with them. It's a quiet flame that keeps burning, something each will carry. As they sit there, breathing together one last time, they both feel it: This isn't an ending. It's a promise. Even in silence, their love lives on.

A Love's Resistant Symphony

In the quiet of your hand against mine,
our fingers find the path they were always meant to trace.
Each touch is a song, a rhythm only our hearts understand,
a melody played by the stars above and the earth below.
Your hand fits into mine,
as though the universe had sculpted it in secret,
a perfect curve, a place where all things are born
and all things are eternal.
Our palms touch and tremble,
like the delicate tremor of a leaf in the wind,
and I know that love is not just a word,
but a thousand stories told in the pulse of our skin.

THE LAST BREATH OF A LOVE

We are two bodies,
but your warmth is already my skin,
and I carry your breath like a river in my chest.
Our hands speak in silence,
a language so ancient it's woven into the bones of our ancestors.
The spaces between our fingers are not empty,
but filled with the weight of every unspoken vow,
the weight of a love so deep,
it presses against the edges of the sky.
In this touch,
I find more than touch—
I find all the names I ever called out to the moon,
and all the whispers I made to the stars.
And here, in the quiet fusion of our hands,
I see the world as it was meant to be—
a love eternal,
our souls braided together in the silent rhythm of time.

Love's Timeless Splendor

In the depths of our love,
a sanctuary grows like a wild flower,
its petals unfolding in the silence of the night.
Here, where souls entwine
in a single breath,
we walk through time,
holding hands,
our love unbroken,
unshaken by the winds that age the world.

I see you,
and in you, I see the light of the earth,
the soft rhythm of the sun's first kiss on the horizon.

THE LAST BREATH OF A LOVE

You are the river,
and I am the stone
waiting to be shaped by your current,
waiting to be molded by your beauty,
a beauty so deep it lives in the bones of the stars.
Nature bows to your allure,
your presence a symphony the mountains whisper to the sea.
Your spirit hums like the first song the wind ever sang,
and I stand before you,
speechless,
lost in the melody of your form.
Oh, how your virtues grow,
like the roses that bloom in the heart of the earth.
Each petal a promise,
each fragrance a prayer,
each gaze a secret
only the soul can understand.
In your eyes, I see a world I have never known—
a place where love is endless,
where it holds me in its arms,
unafraid and wild.
In this love,
we are eternal.
Our bodies touch,
but our souls soar
beyond the borders of time and space,
where nothing can break us.
Your love blooms,
unchanging,
unfading,
a testament to the fire that burns in us
forever.

Stolen Kisses

Under the silver gaze of the moon,
our lips meet in stolen silence,
whispers trembling in the air,
fingers brushing the edges of time.
We are thieves,
but what we steal is the very breath of love,
held between us like a secret
only the stars are meant to hear.

In the dark, your kiss is a flame

THE LAST BREATH OF A LOVE

that melts the hours,
and with each stolen touch,
the world disappears.
We are shadows,
carried on the breeze of desire,
our hearts whispering to each other
in a language no one else can speak.
Your eyes—
they seek me out in the crowd of the world,
and when our gazes meet,
it's as if the earth bends closer,
as if the sea leans in to listen.
Each glance,
each stolen moment between us,
is a promise wrapped in moonlight,
a vow made in silence,
heard only by the night.
Oh, the heat of your kiss—
it burns like fire on my skin,
but it is the kind of fire
that makes the soul dance,
that makes the universe bend in our favor.
We are not just lovers,
but dreamers stealing fragments of time,
pieces of forever caught
in the depths of each kiss,
each trembling touch.
And in these stolen moments,
we are infinite.
The world may break and the stars may fall,
but nothing will ever erase
the imprint of your kiss on my lips,

the echo of your love in my veins.
In these stolen breaths,
we are bound together,
forever and always.

Eternal Embrace

Under the pale light of twilight,
we are one,
our souls twined like vines in the quiet of the night.
In the space between our hearts,
a world is born—
a world where love is the only truth,
and eternity is nothing more than this moment,
this breath we share.

In our eternal embrace,
time shatters,
splintering like glass,
and the stars themselves lean closer
to hear the song of our hearts beating,
a rhythm carved from the bones of the earth.
Our bodies are fire,
our touch is the wind—
we burn together,
we rise together,

our love a flame that dances,
that never dims.
I find shelter in the hollow of your arms,
a sanctuary made of nothing but you and me,
where the world cannot touch us,
where worries fall away like dust in the wind.
Your touch is sacred,
your kiss is a prayer,
and in your embrace,
I find all the warmth
the universe could ever offer.
We move in the rhythm of the night,
our bodies speaking a language older than words.
In this embrace, we are free,
no boundaries can bind us,
no distance can separate us.
We are eternal,
a love that wraps itself around us,
holding us close,
closer than the sun holds the sky.
Through the storms, through the silence,
we weather the passage of time,
our love a tether,
a rope woven from the threads of the stars.
In your arms, I find peace,
I find strength,
a love that does not fade
but grows with every breath we take,
grows as the moon grows full in the night.
In every moment, our souls fuse,
and the depth of this love
is too vast to speak—

it is divine,
it is written in the pulse of the earth,
in the stars that burn above us.
In your embrace, I am whole,
a story told in kisses,
a promise sealed by the universe itself.
Let our hearts remain bound forever,
in this eternal embrace,
where love will endure
long after the world crumbles to dust,
a flame that will never die,
forever pure,
forever ours.

Eyes of Love

When I look into your eyes,
it is as though the world holds its breath.
A storm stirs inside me,
a symphony of stars,
each note vibrating in the hollow of my chest.
Your gaze,
it is a quiet storm,
tender and fierce,
like a river that flows through my soul.

Each time our eyes meet,
I fall a little further—
not with my feet,
but with my heart,
surrendering to the pull of your gaze,
to the depth of that infinite ocean
where I drown and breathe at once.
In the mirror of your eyes,
I see all the stories we have not yet told,
a love that is both ancient and new,
a tale written in the language of fire and silence.
Within those eyes,
I see a world that has never been,
a universe we build with every glance,
with every flicker of light that dances on your lashes,
a constellation where we are both the sky and the stars.
Your eyes—
they hold the night,
and in them, I see the dawn breaking,
as though the sun itself rises from the warmth of your gaze.
Each glance you give me
is a paradise I never knew,
where love blooms wild,
untamed by time,
and where we need not speak,
for the world has already heard our hearts.
With every look,
I fall deeper—
not with words,
but in silence,
enchanted by the promise held in your eyes,
the unspoken love that glimmers there,

tender, infinite.
In your gaze,
I find my peace,
a solace so deep,
it is as though I have been waiting for this moment
for centuries,
for lifetimes.
Each time our eyes meet,
it is as if the earth shifts,
and in your eyes,
I am home.

A Melody of Love's Resilience

Each beat of my heart is a wound,
a rhythm carved from the silence between us,
each thump a shadow of your absence,
a hollow sound that calls your name in vain.
This is the song of my soul—
not a melody of joy,
but a requiem for what we once were.

Through the dark corridors of my chest,
the echoes stretch,
they twist like the wind through the branches of a forgotten tree,

and I am left,
listening to the song of longing,
the anthem of sorrow that beats in me.
It is a rhythm we made together,
now a ghost that dances alone in the ruins.

Every pulse I feel is a bitter memory,
each beat etched with the imprint of your touch,
each rhythm stained with the sweetness of love
that has now slipped through my fingers,
like sand in the dark.
But even in this vast emptiness,
there is something that refuses to break,
a quiet strength that rises from the ashes,
from the brokenness,
a resilience that refuses to die.
I dance with this pain,
its edges sharp as the night,
but it is the dance of a survivor,
of one who has loved too deeply
and has learned to stand again
on the bones of love's absence.

Whispers of a Lost Love

In the silence of my solitude,
whispers stir the air,
like ghosts of a love that once burned bright,
now fading into the shadows of memory.
They are soft,
these whispers,
as soft as the touch of your hand
before it slipped away—
a breeze passing through a broken window.

Oh, how they tease me,
these whispers that curl around my soul,
reminding me of a love
that slipped through my grasp
like the rain through the earth,

THE LAST BREATH OF A LOVE

too quick to catch,
too fleeting to hold.
I reach for the fragments—
they scatter in my hands,
a handful of nothing,
a story untold,
lost in the folds of time.
I call your name to the wind,
but it only answers in silence,
and the space between us grows colder,
wider,
a chasm filled with the echoes of what was.
In the hollow of my chest,
where your presence used to live,
there is only the faint echo of a kiss,
a memory that stirs in the dark.
The whispers cling to me,
like the scent of a flower that once bloomed
but now has withered,
and I strain to hear them—
but they are a song sung by a distant sea,
and I cannot reach it.
Yet, in this quiet despair,
there is a strange grace—
for even as the love slips away,
even as it falls like sand between my fingers,
these whispers remain.
They remind me,
not of the pain,
but of the grandness of what we had—
a love that was once vast,
and is now just a whisper in the wind.

Echoes of Love

The echoes of our love drift through the air,
soft as the twilight,
and they haunt me,
whispering the memory of a love
that was once infinite,
now just a shadow on the wind.
Your laughter,
like the song of distant birds,
rises and falls,
carrying with it both joy and sorrow,
the touch of something lost,
yet still so vivid.

THE LAST BREATH OF A LOVE

In the stillness,
when the world is hushed,
I hear them—
the echoes of our love,
deep and unyielding,
reverberating through the empty spaces of my soul.
They move within me,
a melody that both heals and wounds,
a bittersweet refrain
that drifts like smoke,
carrying the weight of everything we were.
Your voice,
once the pulse of my heart,
now a murmur in the dark,
speaks of what we had,
the warmth of your touch,
the sweetness of our kiss.
But even your whispers tremble now,
fragile as the moon's light on the sea,
and the warmth we shared fades
like the sun sinking into the horizon,
slowly,
silently.
The echoes stretch and twist,
and as they fade,
they leave me with a longing,
a hollow ache
where your presence once lived.
Still, I hold them—
these echoes,
clinging to their remnants,
for in their quiet I find you again.

Our love does not die,
it lingers here,
within the breath of every passing moment.
Though the echoes may wear thin,
they carry the soul of our love,
a love that was once wild and unbroken,
now wrapped in the softness of memories.
They are the essence of us—
the time we spent,
the tenderness we shared,
our connection carved into the silence of the world,
forever enshrined
in the echoes of love.

Heart's Scars

The scars upon my heart,
they are a map,
a map drawn in blood and fire,
each mark a testament
to a love that once burned
with the ferocity of a sun too close to the earth.
These scars are not just wounds,
but stories—
of passion that rose like a wave,
of moments when we were everything and nothing,
of vulnerability laid bare beneath the weight of desire.
They are the echo of love's true voice,
its whisper and its roar.

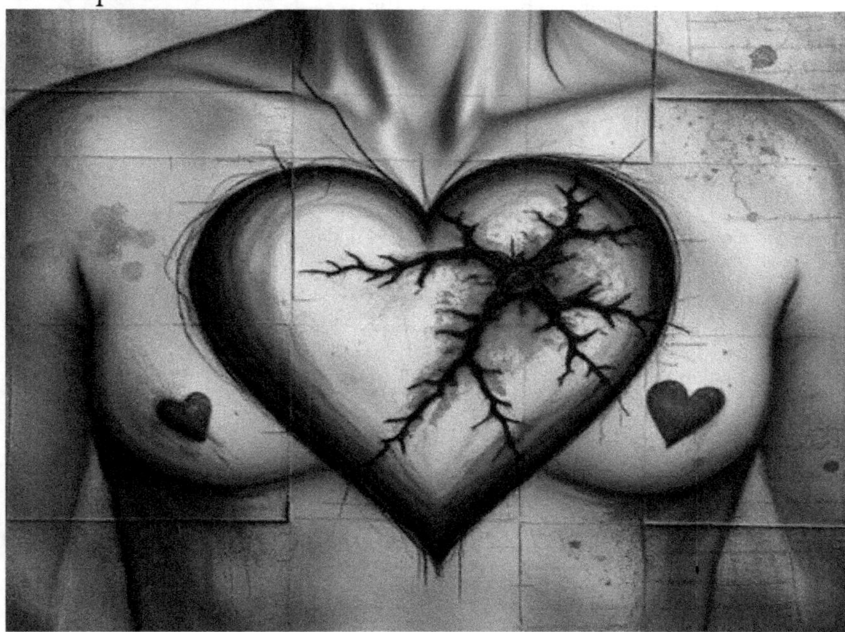

Each scar is a deep imprint,

etched by the hands of time and tenderness,
witnessing the depth of my soul's yearning,
my willingness to be torn apart
and put together again.
They are the marks of courage,
of the daring to love
when the world threatens to break you,
to stand with open arms
even when the storm clouds darken.
In each line carved into my chest,
I find not just pain,
but strength that rises from the earth itself,
roots growing deeper,
stronger,
through the cracks of my being.
For love is not without its brilliance—
its intricate light is woven into every scar,
its beauty resides in the fragility of the heart.
These scars are not solely sorrowful—
they carry the weight of love's marrow,
its deepest truth,
its unspoken promise.
They remind me that healing is not a simple thing,
but a resurrection,
a rebirth from the very place where the heart bled.
And in this space,
love's wounds become a mirror—
reflecting the soul's hidden strength,
revealing the profound depths of what it means to love.

Tears of Release

With each tear that falls,
I let go of a piece of myself,
as though the earth itself were crying through me.
Each drop, heavy with the weight of what was,
a fragment of a love that still lingers in the silence of my chest.
These tears carry the essence of our time,
the sweetness and the sting,
and in their flow,
they whisper of a love once vast,
now soft as the evening's last light.

As they fall,
these tears cleanse the broken parts of me,
they cleanse the pain and open the spaces
where healing can dance.
They carve a river through my soul,
a river that carries all the sorrows
of a love that has passed,
and still,
I feel its warmth lingering,
like the last breath of a summer wind.
Each tear,
it is a prayer,

THE LAST BREATH OF A LOVE

a soft prayer for release,
for the courage to let go of what no longer lives,
to surrender the weight of what once held me,
to learn to ebb and flow with the rhythm of life.
With every drop,
I shed a skin of memories,
each layer falling away,
leaving behind only what remains—
a heart that, though scarred,
beats with a tenderness that will not fade.
For within these tears,
there is a grace,
a quiet grace that speaks without words,
that tells me love is never lost,
only transformed.
I honor each tear that falls,
for in its descent,
I find my strength,
my ability to release what once clung to me
and embrace the love that still pulses
in the dark corners of my soul.
For in the heart's vulnerability,
I find my truth—
a love that cannot be shaken,
a love that, though it fades,
never truly leaves.

Canvas of Longing

You were my muse,
the flame that flickered within me,
the pulse behind my words,
the spark that made my heart beat in verses.
In your presence,
I found the canvas of my soul,
and every line I wrote
was a testament to the love you gave me.

But now,

THE LAST BREATH OF A LOVE

your absence paints my world in shadows—
a landscape of sorrow,
where the colors bleed into each other,
blue and gray,
as though the very sky wept for us.
My hand falters,
the pen quivers in my grasp,
seeking the echo of your touch,
longing for the fire that once blazed so brightly.
In every word I write,
your spirit slips away like sand,
the once steady river of thought
now a dry well,
cracked and empty.
The ink no longer flows
but stumbles like footsteps in a forgotten path,
seeking the rhythm that your presence once gave.
Yet, in this sorrow,
I find a strange peace—
for even in your absence,
you are still here,
in every line, in every pause,
your memory carved into the marrow of my poems.
Each stroke of pain is a monument,
a tribute to the love we shared,
that beautiful love,
now softened by time,
but never erased.
Though the tears may fall,
I will write our story,
beneath the weight of the moon,
where the stars tremble in silence,

and the night listens to the echoes of our past.
For even in the sorrow,
love remains—
etched into the canvas of my heart,
forever immortal.
You were my muse,
and though you have gone,
your spirit endures—
alive in every verse I write,
in every word I sing.
And as I paint this canvas with the colors of loss,
I will hold close the love we once knew,
a love that lives beyond the brushstrokes,
a love that will never fade.

Love's Legacy in Bittersweet Memories

The love we once carried,
like a flame delicate and wild,
now flickers in the hollows of memory,
etched into the bones of my soul,
its light soft but unyielding.
In the shadows of my heart,
your image lingers,
whispering its truth in the quiet spaces of time.

In the endless corridors of my thoughts,

you walk,
a presence that cannot be forgotten,
a breath I still feel on my skin,
even as the years pull us apart.
Each moment we shared
is now a treasure I guard
with trembling hands—
a touch that neither time nor distance
can erase.
How I ache to turn back the hours,
to hold you again in the world we once knew,
where your love was a sun that warmed my every shadow.
But destiny, cruel and silent,
with its twisting paths,
has taken you away,
leaving me with these ghosts,
these memories,
to hold in your place.
I cherish the moments—
the laughter, the silence, the tears—
for in their depths,
I find the essence of our love,
its pulse still beating in the dark,
as strong as the day it was born.
Though you have gone,
the fabric of us remains—
woven into every thought,
every sigh,
every breath I take.
And so, I hold you—
in the bittersweet embrace of memory,
knowing that your love leaves its mark,

its eternal trace,
written not in the sands of time,
but in the chambers of my heart,
where it will never fade.
For what we shared,
though now a shadow,
still shines—
an indelible light,
a love that will never vanish.

Aching Void, Enduring Love

After you left, my love,
I fell into the void—
a dark wound in my chest,
a cavern without echo or light.
No solace came,
no voice from above,
only the silence that followed
your absence,
a silence as vast as the ocean,
swallowing everything,
leaving me alone.

THE LAST BREATH OF A LOVE

Your touch,
once a breeze that soothed my skin,
is now a phantom,
whispering in the corners of my memory.
The warmth we shared
now a fading star,
its light scattered,
leaving me adrift,
floating on a sea of longing.
No words can heal
the wound carved deep within me,
no other love can fill

the hollow you left behind.
In this immense emptiness,
I ache with unrest,
yearning for the days when we were whole,
when you were here,
and I was whole in your presence.
Yet, even in this darkness,
a flicker stirs—
a breath,
a spark of light
from the remnants of our love.
For love, my love,
is a force that does not die,
a flame that flickers even when the wind howls.
And though you are gone,
the memory of us
lives on in the marrow of my bones.
I see you in the spaces between breaths,
in the spaces between moments,
in the lingering scent of you that I carry.
Your love is an imprint,
a mark upon my soul,
that time cannot erase.
The moments we shared,
the laughter, the quiet,
the softness of your voice,
they are written on me,
etched forever in the fabric of my being.
Even as I sink into this aching void,
I know—
I know, beyond the shadow of despair—
that love endures.

THE LAST BREATH OF A LOVE

It cannot be taken,
it cannot be undone.
The love we had is a river
that runs through me,
forever alive,
forever faithful.

Your Laughter, the Symphony of Joy

Your laughter, beloved,
    is a song without end,
    a wild and untamed symphony,
    unfolding like the wind's first breath,
    spreading through the air,
    sweeping across the earth,
    a melody that knows no limits,
    no boundaries.

In its notes,
I find peace—
not the quiet kind,
but a storm of light,
a river of sound
that cleanses the dust from my heart,
that softens the rough edges of my soul.

THE LAST BREATH OF A LOVE

It falls like rain,
like the sun that rises after the night,
filling every crevice with warmth,
turning the ordinary into the sacred.
Each burst of your joy,
each explosion of laughter,
resonates deep within my chest—
a pulse that stirs the bones,
that sings the song of my own heart.
It spreads across the fields of my spirit,
igniting flames,
awakening the dormant parts of me,
until I too,
laugh without knowing why.
Your laughter,
a storm that cannot be contained,
a river that carves its own path,
is a language the earth knows.
It calls the mountains to dance,
the oceans to rise.
In it, I find my sanctuary—
a refuge where the world's burdens
disappear like mist at dawn.
Oh, how it fills the air,
like the scent of rain,
like the call of a bird
lifting from the earth into the sky.
Your laughter, dear,
is a song carved into the heavens,
a melody that lingers
long after the sound has gone.
It is the pulse of life,

the heartbeat of the world,
the voice of joy that does not know sorrow—
forever rising,
forever unbroken,
forever mine.

Under the Moon

Beneath the moon, we lie—
our bodies tangled,
our hearts beating in the same rhythm,
the earth beneath us,
the heavens above.
The stars, like scattered fragments of forgotten dreams,
dance around us,
whispering secrets we will never know.

The moon's light touches your skin,

a silken caress,
and I am lost in the grace of your face,
as if the universe itself
had taken form in you.
In the stillness,
time crumbles into dust—
the hours scatter like petals in the wind,
and we are left in this perfect moment,
together,
alone,
one.
We speak in whispers,
words that are born not of the mouth,
but of the soul,
each laugh a note in the symphony of our love.
The moon listens,
its pale glow a witness to our joy,
its silver fingers tracing the edges of our skin
as we create memories
that will never age.
Under this sky,
our love swells and deepens,
rooted in the night,
strong as the mountains,
as inevitable as the dawn.
With your hand in mine,
we are no longer two—
we are a single breath,
a single heartbeat,
a single shadow.

The Absence We Share

I search for you in the folds of night,
where shadows coil like forgotten dreams,
but find only silence,
a vast silence
that fills the cracks in my soul.
Your name still trembles on my lips,
a fragile echo that fades before the dawn,
and yet it clings to the marrow of my bones,
like a fire that burns but cannot consume.
The absence of your touch
is a wound that does not heal,
a thirst that no river can quench.

I loved you with the fullness of my skin,
each heartbeat a pulse of our shared breath,
each glance a poem we wrote
without words,
without need of language.
You were my language,
the syllables of joy in my mouth,
the salt of my tears.
Now, I walk through a landscape of memory,
a desolate field where your voice once bloomed.
I hold the air between my hands,
trying to grasp what has slipped through me,
like sand slipping through the fingers of a dying sun.
And yet, I do not mourn,

THE LAST BREATH OF A LOVE

for to mourn is to surrender
to the passing of what was never truly ours.
I will never surrender to you,
nor to the empty space where your love used to be.
You are not gone,
you are a part of the stars that spill across my sky,
a part of the earth that holds my sorrow.
In the curve of the moon's light,
I still feel the weight of your absence,
the weight of love that lingers
long after it has been lost.
I search for you in the folds of night,
and when I do not find you,
I realize—
I am not searching for your body,
but for the heart
that once beat inside of mine.

The Weight of You

I carry you in the hollow of my chest,
like a wound that refuses to close.
You are the rhythm of my breath,
the pulse between my ribs,
a song that is sung without melody.

Every corner of this house
still trembles with your name,
as though the walls themselves
have been shaped by the echo of your voice.
I walk through rooms you once filled,

THE LAST BREATH OF A LOVE

and I reach out,
but your touch is only the dust
that settles where you stood.
You were the fire that burned my tongue,
the sweetness that turned to salt in my mouth.
I thought I could hold you forever,
but you slipped like water through my hands,
like the promises we whispered
beneath the skin of the stars.
I remember the sound of your laughter,
the way it cut through the silence of my nights,
like a blade of light,
sharp and tender,
a melody too perfect to be true.
And now, your silence fills the room,
heavy and thick,
like a cloud that refuses to break.
I wait for you in the folds of the dawn,
where the sun touches the earth,
but all I find is the hollow place
where you once were.
Your absence is a country I have learned to live in,
but it does not speak to me.
It only holds me,
shackled to the memory of what we were.
I write your name in the dust of my sorrow,
I carve it into the soil where flowers once grew.
Your name is the only thing that remains
of the garden we built in the heat of our love.
But it is not enough.
It never will be enough.
For your love was a river,

and now I am left with the dry riverbed,
cracked and parched,
waiting for the flood
that will never come.
Still, I carry you,
in the deepest parts of me,
where no light can reach,
where the weight of you presses on my chest,
and I cannot breathe without it.
You were my air,
my breath,
my skin,
and now,
you are the shadow that follows me,
the storm I cannot escape.
And though you are gone,
you are here,
always here,
the unspoken wound in my soul,
the absence I cannot name,
the love that does not end,
but stays
and stays
and stays.

The Silence Left by You

I wake to the sound of your absence,
a silence that fills the room like smoke,
thick, suffocating,
pressing against the walls of my chest.
You are no longer here,
and yet,
your absence is all that remains.

I try to call your name,
but it shatters in the air,
a broken syllable,
a cry that cannot reach the sky.
Where have you gone?

SAGOR SARKER

Where has the warmth of your voice hidden itself?
Where is the love that once burned
so fiercely in the spaces between us?
Now, only echoes remain—
empty echoes that bounce off the walls of my heart.
I remember your touch—
how it once traced the contours of my soul,
as if you were a part of me,
woven into the fabric of my skin.
But now, your touch is a ghost,
a fading memory that slips through my fingers,
like water running from the cracks of my hands.
The bed is cold without you,
the sheets lie still, untouched,
waiting for the warmth of your body
that will never come again.
I sleep in the hollow space you left,
but even in dreams,
I find no rest,
only your shadow,
lurking in the corners of my mind.
I cannot reach you,
cannot hold you in the way I once did.
All that is left is the fading trace
of your breath on my skin,
the last kiss that was never meant to be the last.
You left me with no farewell,
no promise of return—
only the weight of your absence,
that sinks deeper with each passing day.
I loved you so completely,
with every part of me,

THE LAST BREATH OF A LOVE

and now,
I am left to grieve the love that was never finished,
the love that was cut too soon,
like a flower torn from its roots.
You were my world,
and now my world is just an endless night
where the stars do not shine
and the moon is a hollow mirror,
reflecting only my sorrow.
I walk through the days,
a body without purpose,
a shadow without a soul,
for you were my breath,
my reason,
and now I am nothing without you.
In the silence of the hours,
I try to remember what it was like
to be whole—
to feel the pulse of life in my veins,
but I only feel the absence of you,
deep, cavernous,
infallible.
You are gone,
but you remain,
a wound that will never heal,
a cry that will never stop echoing.
And I wonder,
do you feel this pain too,
in some distant place,
or have you forgotten
the love we shared?
Have you left it behind

as you walked away,
leaving me here,
a prisoner of the silence
you left in your wake?

Shadows of You

I search for you in the shadows,
in the spaces between the hours,
where your scent lingers like forgotten rain.
I cannot see you,
but your absence is a presence I cannot escape.
I have walked through every corner of this house,
each step echoing with the memory of your name.
The walls that once held your laughter now stand silent,
their whispers the only sound I hear.

Where are you, love?
Where are the words we spoke beneath the moon,
the dreams we wove together,

now scattered like ash in the wind?
I grasp at fragments of you—
pieces of your touch,
the warmth of your embrace—but they slip away,
like water through my hands.
In the darkness, I wait,
but you never return.
Your absence is a wound that bleeds
whenever I close my eyes.

Beneath the Fallen Stars

I lay beneath the fallen stars,
my hands reaching toward a sky emptied of you.
Each star is a memory, faint embers scattered,
flames that once blazed and now lie cold,
fading, drifting from my heart.

I would give my life to bring you back,
to feel the warmth of your breath,
to hear your voice melt into the quiet night.
But the heavens are silent, indifferent,

casting their cold light on a world that has never known
the hollow ache of losing a love like ours.
You were fire in my veins,
the song that rose in my blood,
and now, I wander through this life,
a shadow of the man I was,
haunted by the silence you've left behind.

The Weight of Absence

Each day, I bear the weight of your absence,
a burden that presses heavier than mountains.
In the morning, the sun rises—cold, indifferent—
and I face the hours, each one dragging behind me
like footsteps sinking in the snow.

I remember how your eyes would spark with light,
how they caught the stars and held them,
how, when you looked at me, even the night softened.
But now, those eyes are lost to me,
leaving only the memory of their warmth.
Now I am left in this cold that never relents.
I try to fill the silence with words,

but no sound can reach the hollow carved in my chest.
I speak your name, hoping it might echo,
that somehow it will find you.
But it fades, a forgotten prayer cast into the dark—
unanswered, unheard, lost forever.

When You Left

When you left,
the world became a land without light.
No song could touch my ears,
no color could reach my eyes,
for you took the sun with you,
and left me wrapped in shadow.
I wander through the streets we walked together,
each step pressing into the hollow of what we once shared.
Now the ground is mine alone,
an empty path beneath my feet.

I would give all that I am to hear your voice again,
to feel the warmth of your hand in mine.
But you are gone,
and I am left tracing the ghost of you,
finding only echoes of your touch

in every corner of this earth.

The Absence of Your Touch

Your touch was once the warmth
that softened every fear,
the light that carried me through storms.
But now, your hands are distant, beyond reach,
and I am left in the cold shadows
that stretch longer as night falls.

In my dreams, I reach for you,
but your touch slips from my grasp,
like the last breath of the setting sun.
I wake to a world that has turned to ice,
my body aching, followed by the space you left.
Yet, you are in every thought,
woven into every breath,
a presence that will not fade,

a love that endures,
even when you are no longer here.

Gentle Currents

The sky grows black, the clouds rise high,
a tempest stirs, ominous and sly.
The wind begins to moan and wail,
as stormy lines in darkness trail.
A flash of lightning, sharp and bright,
tears through the veil of creeping night.
Thunder rolls like the devil's breath,
as stormy lines charge toward their death.

The rain descends in furious sheets,
each drop a ghost, each wave repeats.
The stormy lines crash, claw, and rave,
a madness born from ocean's grave.
The trees bow low, their branches sway,

as stormy lines carve out their way.
Nature's wrath laid bare to see,
its voice—a twisted symphony.
Yet as the stormy lines recede,
a gentler force begins to lead.
A spectral rainbow haunts the sky,
and stormy lines bid their goodbye.
For in the heart of dark despair,
a beauty stirs, unseen, laid bare.
So let us greet the stormy lines,
for even shadows hold designs.

Whispers of the Rain

As the night of rain descends, so cold,
The silence breaks, and shadows unfold.
The raindrops, like a mournful choir,
Whisper secrets of a soul's desire.
Each drop—a sigh, a fleeting breath,
A symbol of love, entwined with death.
It touches all with gentle grace,
Yet washes away what time can't erase.

Our love, like rain, falls soft and deep,
Cleansing the wounds that we cannot keep.
In the stillness, our hearts align,
As each drop falls, our spirits entwine.

SAGOR SARKER

We listen to the rain's soft song,
A melody that lingers long.
With every beat, our hearts beat true,
As we pause, in the silence, just me and you.
The night is heavy with whispered dreams,
A realm where love and longing gleams.
We dance beneath the sorrowed sky,
Two souls, alone, yet soaring high.
Let the rain fall, relentless and wild,
For in its dark embrace, we are beguiled.
In this night, where shadows creep,
We are bound in a love that shall never sleep.

Sunlit Hearts

The sun hangs low, a spectral flame,
And in its glow, I speak thy name.
A fleeting love, yet boundless, deep,
A passion that shall never sleep.
The warmth upon my skin, thy hand,
A story carved upon the sand.
A moment caught in time's cruel grip,
A love that trembles, slow and swift.

The ocean's voice, a mournful cry,
The winds that whisper, passing by.

SAGOR SARKER

In thine embrace, I find my peace,
A fleeting joy that shall not cease.
Like flowers blooming 'Neath the sun,
Our love takes root, though we're undone.
The beauty of the world around,
Is mirrored in the love we've found.
But lo, this summer love must fade,
As shadows lengthen, light must trade.
Yet still, I hear the silent plea—
A love that lingers, haunting me.
So let us clasp this moment tight,
In darkness bound, in fading light.
For though the summer's fire may die,
In this, our hearts shall never cry.

Dancing with the Stars

Her beauty in motion, a vision divine,
A sight that steals breath, yet time cannot bind.
Like a breeze on the lake, soft and unbound,
Her graceful dance makes my soul rebound.
Each step, each turn, a delicate flight,
A rhythm that stirs the deepest night.
Her beauty, like poetry, pure and sweet,
A love that endures with each heartbeat.

How she says, like branches in bloom,
Her dance dispels all sorrow, all gloom.
Her beauty in motion, a truth to hold,
A love that, like nature, is timeless and bold.
With ease she moves, as though the air

Holds her gently, with no weight to bear.
Her beauty in motion, serene, complete,
A love that is endless, both quiet and fleet.
So let us dance 'Neath the moon's soft light,
And let our love be the stars in the night.
For in her beauty, with each graceful move,
Lies the reason why my heart seeks to prove.

Always in Bloom

If you forget me, let it be swift,
As the sunset's glow begins to lift,
Like a fleeting shadow on the shore,
A whispered sigh that's heard no more.
If you forget me, let it be light,
Like a star that fades into the night,
Like the embers of a fire's glow,
Dimming softly as the winds do blow.

If you forget me, let it be calm,
Like the sea at dusk, a peaceful balm,
Like the snow that falls in quiet grace,
A soft, pale veil that time can't erase.
If you forget me, let it be still,

Like the last breath, a final will,
Like the sunset's slow, fading hue,
A departure known, and then passed through.
But if you remember, let it be true,
Like the dawn that paints the sky anew,
Like a flower that opens in the morn,
And with each petal, fresh hope is born.
For though you may forget, my love shall stay,
Unyielding, like the earth's embrace each day.
Like a forget-me-not, gentle and mild,
Blooming evermore, forever beguiled.

You break my heart

You shatter my heart, love, with a blow so fierce
that even silence feels torn and coarse.
I carry this wound like an ember in my chest,
a flame that won't dim, that I can't release.
In the ruins of our dreams, where warmth once stirred,
only shadows linger, broken and blurred.
Your absence haunts the hollows of my days—
a voice gone silent in love's vast space.

The laughter we once knew, it fades and falls
like the notes of a song played behind distant walls.
What once pulsed with life now chills and fades,
a once-blooming flower now lost in the shade.
The ghost of your touch still clings to my skin,

a sharp and stinging reminder within.
Those promises—fragile, brittle as glass—
splinter and scatter, with scars left to amass.
With each breath, my heart feels heavier yet,
as if it must bear the weight of regret.
Tears carve deep rivers down my soul's face,
a sorrow that time can neither cleanse nor erase.
But somewhere, beyond this shadowed place,
I'll reach for the light and rebuild my grace.
For hearts that break can yet learn to rise,
gathering strength like stars from night skies.
Yes, you've broken my heart, but not my soul—
through this ache, I'll find a new whole.
In the belly of pain, I'll seek and I'll see
the worth of a love built on what could be.

What Still Hurts

You've taken something from me,
a soft and glistening part of my soul.
It feels like skin torn raw,
an ache that sits in the hollow of my chest
and whispers its quiet misery, relentless, unfurling.
There is a dead weight in every dawn now,
the sky hangs heavy, thick as smoke.
My hands tremble with emptiness,
touching only shadows where once there was warmth.
I reach, but everything slips, slips—
a thousand shards, sharp, invisible, cold.

My heart is a bruise the color of dusk,
darkening beneath ribs that strain to keep it contained.

SAGOR SARKER

The wound is old but fresh,
a haunted ache that refuses to fade
and sings its broken songs in the night.
Once, there were mornings gilded in gold,
laughter glinting like sunlight on water,
and love that wrapped around us like a soft sheet,
holding all the jagged pieces close,
holding us whole, even when we frayed.
Now I walk through rooms echoing hollow,
a ghost tethered to memories that bite,
and you—you're gone,
yet woven into every moment that cuts.
I dream of silence but wake to noise,
of old promises echoing in endless loops,
their weight pressing me down,
heavy and merciless as the gravity of loss.
How long, I wonder, can a heart break itself?
How much sorrow can a body hold
before it finally shatters into silence,
the way waves wear down stone,
turning even the hardest pieces into sand?
But in this dark, I still breathe,
as if survival were a spiteful act,
a kind of stubborn light.
And though I ache, though I bleed,
there is a pulse beneath all this rubble.
Maybe one day, that will be enough.

An Elegy for What Was

It's all broken glass and bone here,
a barren field where we once planted dreams,
where love was soft and green, spilling over
like water that never thought to end.
Now each breath feels like rust,
a slow decay that fills the lungs,
heavy, scraping down to the hollow core
where something tender once beat, unafraid.

You left fingerprints on everything I am,
in the quiet, in the cracked light of dawn.
They haunt the walls, these shadows of you,
like ghosts who refuse to leave,

like names whispered through endless fog.
Every word you spoke still breathes inside me,
but thin and faded, like echoes in snow.
I cup them in my hands, fragile relics
that melt in my grasp, slipping back to silence.
There was a time I knew joy like fire,
bright and warm, as if we could burn
through all the darkness that stretched around us.
Now, it's just me, hands trembling in cold rooms,
touching only the memory of flame.
Is there a limit to what a heart can hold?
Or do we keep piling ache upon ache,
like stones stacked in grief's quiet ritual,
each one heavier, pulling us down?
I search for your face in empty places,
in mirrors, in windows at dusk,
trying to understand where you went,
how you could slip from this world of mine,
leaving me a sky too vast and too silent.
I speak to the shadows sometimes,
just to hear the sound of a voice,
but it's empty, hollow as the space you left.
And still, I breathe, as if this weight
could somehow hold me up.

Where the Silence Lives

It's in the quiet now, the weight of you,
pressing into empty rooms, settling like dust.
There are echoes that breathe in the walls,
old laughter caught in the seams, frayed
and fading, but refusing to go.
I wander through these hollowed-out days,
arms reaching for what isn't there,
like fingers grasping at smoke,
finding nothing but the sting of air.
I am empty hands, trembling with memory,
a vessel poured out, still aching to fill.

Once, there was warmth in my chest,
a spark that you fed with every smile,

every whispered word in the dark.
Now, the spark is ash—
it gathers in my throat like unspoken grief,
a heaviness I can neither swallow nor release.
I trace the shape of you in everything,
in old letters, in forgotten clothes,
in the faint perfume that clings like a shadow
to the door you left behind.
It's strange how absence can grow so large,
taking up space, filling rooms with its vastness,
like a tide that rises and drowns all sound.
Nights are the hardest, stretched too long,
where seconds drip down like slow rain.
The dark wraps around me, tight and cold,
and I press my hand to the sheets you've left bare,
as if warmth might somehow return,
as if love could stay bound to an empty space.
I wonder if you feel this too—
the ache that lives like a pulse in silence,
a beating wound that never heals,
that only deepens, widening the divide.
Are you somewhere out there, whole, untouched,
while I unravel, thread by fragile thread,
a tapestry torn and scattered on the wind?
I carry you in each hollow breath,
a burden and a solace both.
You are the weight that grounds me,
the ache that reminds me I'm alive,
and the dream I wake from, reaching into night,
only to find a handful of empty air.
Maybe someday I'll let you go,
release you like sand slipping through fingers,

watching each grain fall back to earth.
But for now, you are my ghost, my shadow,
the absence that clings, stubborn as love,
and I am the one left behind, still breathing.

A Hunger for What's Gone

You left me a house of dust and bones,
hollow rooms where only the wind moves.
There's a hunger here, sharp and unyielding,
a hollow ache that echoes and grows,
as if loss itself could have teeth,
could gnaw its way into my marrow.
Every corner holds a memory,
every silence waits for your voice,
each one an uninvited guest, lingering,
pulling me back to when we were whole—
before love became an echo, a bruise,
before it cracked open and drained away.

I wear grief like an old coat, heavy,

its weight sinking into my shoulders,
its threads woven with whispered names,
lost promises that rattle like bones.
I wrap myself in it, this quiet agony,
as if it could bring me closer to you.
There's a stillness in the mornings now,
a cold clarity where warmth used to be.
I pour coffee for one,
watch steam spiral and vanish,
just as your breath did beside me,
just as you vanished without warning.
Nights are worse, when shadows deepen,
when even the moon seems to know
the shape of what's missing,
its pale light casting ghosts on the walls.
I lie awake, counting moments we lost,
whispering questions to an empty room,
waiting for answers that never come.
I wonder if I'll ever forget the sound
of your laughter, the warmth of your touch—
or if these fragments are stitched too deep,
woven into the fabric of who I am,
etched into my bones like scars.
And yet, there's a flicker, stubborn and small,
some whisper of hope, or maybe defiance,
that says I'll rise from this hollow place,
that I'll find a way to carry the weight,
that I'll hold the memory of you
without letting it hollow me whole.

An Elegy for What Was

It's all broken glass and bone here,
a barren field where we once planted dreams,
where love was soft and green, spilling over
like water that never thought to end.
Now each breath feels like rust,
a slow decay that fills the lungs,
heavy, scraping down to the hollow core
where something tender once beat, unafraid.

You left fingerprints on everything I am,
in the quiet, in the cracked light of dawn.
They haunt the walls, these shadows of you,
like ghosts who refuse to leave,

like names whispered through endless fog.
Every word you spoke still breathes inside me,
but thin and faded, like echoes in snow.
I cup them in my hands, fragile relics
that melt in my grasp, slipping back to silence.
There was a time I knew joy like fire,
bright and warm, as if we could burn
through all the darkness that stretched around us.
Now, it's just me, hands trembling in cold rooms,
touching only the memory of flame.
Is there a limit to what a heart can hold?
Or do we keep piling ache upon ache,
like stones stacked in grief's quiet ritual,
each one heavier, pulling us down?
I search for your face in empty places,
in mirrors, in windows at dusk,
trying to understand where you went,
how you could slip from this world of mine,
leaving me a sky too vast and too silent.
I speak to the shadows sometimes,
just to hear the sound of a voice,
but it's empty, hollow as the space you left.
And still, I breathe, as if this weight
could somehow hold me up.

Where the Silence Lives

It's in the quiet now, the weight of you,
pressing into empty rooms, settling like dust.
There are echoes that breathe in the walls,
old laughter caught in the seams, frayed
and fading, but refusing to go.
I wander through these hollowed-out days,
arms reaching for what isn't there,
like fingers grasping at smoke,
finding nothing but the sting of air.
I am empty hands, trembling with memory,
a vessel poured out, still aching to fill.

Once, there was warmth in my chest,

THE LAST BREATH OF A LOVE

a spark that you fed with every smile,
every whispered word in the dark.
Now, the spark is ash—
it gathers in my throat like unspoken grief,
a heaviness I can neither swallow nor release.
I trace the shape of you in everything,
in old letters, in forgotten clothes,
in the faint perfume that clings like a shadow
to the door you left behind.
It's strange how absence can grow so large,
taking up space, filling rooms with its vastness,
like a tide that rises and drowns all sound.
Nights are the hardest, stretched too long,
where seconds drip down like slow rain.
The dark wraps around me, tight and cold,
and I press my hand to the sheets you've left bare,
as if warmth might somehow return,
as if love could stay bound to an empty space.
I wonder if you feel this too—
the ache that lives like a pulse in silence,
a beating wound that never heals,
that only deepens, widening the divide.
Are you somewhere out there, whole, untouched,
while I unravel, thread by fragile thread,
a tapestry torn and scattered on the wind?
I carry you in each hollow breath,
a burden and a solace both.
You are the weight that grounds me,
the ache that reminds me I'm alive,
and the dream I wake from, reaching into night,
only to find a handful of empty air.
Maybe someday I'll let you go,

release you like sand slipping through fingers,
watching each grain fall back to earth.
But for now, you are my ghost, my shadow,
the absence that clings, stubborn as love,
and I am the one left behind, still breathing.

A Hunger for What's Gone

You left me a house of dust and bones,
hollow rooms where only the wind moves.
There's a hunger here, sharp and unyielding,
a hollow ache that echoes and grows,
as if loss itself could have teeth,
could gnaw its way into my marrow.
Every corner holds a memory,
every silence waits for your voice,
each one an uninvited guest, lingering,
pulling me back to when we were whole—
before love became an echo, a bruise,
before it cracked open and drained away.

I wear grief like an old coat, heavy,
its weight sinking into my shoulders,

its threads woven with whispered names,
lost promises that rattle like bones.
I wrap myself in it, this quiet agony,
as if it could bring me closer to you.
There's a stillness in the mornings now,
a cold clarity where warmth used to be.
I pour coffee for one,
watch steam spiral and vanish,
just as your breath did beside me,
just as you vanished without warning.
Nights are worse, when shadows deepen,
when even the moon seems to know
the shape of what's missing,
its pale light casting ghosts on the walls.
I lie awake, counting moments we lost,
whispering questions to an empty room,
waiting for answers that never come.
I wonder if I'll ever forget the sound
of your laughter, the warmth of your touch—
or if these fragments are stitched too deep,
woven into the fabric of who I am,
etched into my bones like scars.

END

THE LAST BREATH OF A LOVE

My name is F. N. M. Komor, but most people know me as *Sagor Sarker*. I'm from Bangladesh, a beautiful country in South Asia. Born on 01November , 1990, I have a background in Management, with both graduate and post-graduate degrees, plus an MBA in Marketing.

Writing has always been my passion, even though it's not my profession. I love reading books and exploring new ideas, and I enjoy sharing my thoughts and stories with others. Through my writing, I aim to connect with readers and bring a bit of my world to theirs.

By- Sagor Sarker

fnmkomor@gmail.com

The Last Breath of a Love

For permission requests, please contact the publisher by writing to:

Attention: Permissions Coordinator

Email: fnmkomor@gmail.com

Published by Self-Publishing

Author: Sagor Sarker

ISBN: 9798230831228

About the Author

My name is F. N. M. Komor, but most people know me as *Sagor Sarker*. I'm from Bangladesh, a beautiful country in South Asia. Born on 01November , 1990, I have a background in Management, with both graduate and post-graduate degrees, plus an MBA in Marketing.

Writing has always been my passion, even though it's not my profession. I love reading books and exploring new ideas, and I enjoy sharing my thoughts and stories with others. Through my writing, I aim to connect with readers and bring a bit of my world to theirs.

Read more at https://www.facebook.com/sagor.sarker.334/.

www.ingramcontent.com/pod-product-compliance
Lightning Source LLC
LaVergne TN
LVHW010114170826
845678LV00012B/2408